T0402598

CAREERS IN THE

U.S. COAST GUARD

U. S. COAST GUARD

MILITARY SERVICE

CAREERS IN THE
U.S. COAST GUARD

BY EDWARD F. DOLAN

Marshall Cavendish
Benchmark
New York

Special thanks to Captain Robert C. Ayer, a professor in the Humanities Department at the U.S. Coast Guard Academy, for his review of the manuscript.

MARSHALL CAVENDISH BENCHMARK
99 WHITE PLAINS ROAD
TARRYTOWN, NY 10591
www.marshallcavendish.us

Copyright © 2010 by Marshall Cavendish Corporation

All Internet sites were available and accurate when this book was sent to press.

Library of Congress Cataloging-in-Publication Data

Dolan, Edward F., 1924–
Careers in the U.S. Coast Guard / by Edward F. Dolan.
p. cm. — (Military service)
Includes bibliographical references and index.
Summary: "Discusses service in the U.S. Coast Guard, including training, educational benefits, and career opportunities"—Provided by publisher.
ISBN 978-0-7614-4207-3
1. United States. Coast Guard. 2. United States. Coast Guard—Vocational guidance.
I. Title.
VG53.D65 2008
363.28'602373—dc22
2008039819

EDITOR: Megan Comerford   PUBLISHER: Michelle Bisson
ART DIRECTOR: Anahid Hamparian   SERIES DESIGNER: Kristen Branch / Michael Nelson Design

Photo research by Candlepants Incorporated
Cover photo: PA2 Zac Crawford / U.S. Coast Guard Photo
The photographs in this book are used by permission and through the courtesy of: U.S. Coast Guard Photo: PA3 Connie Terrell, 2–3; PA3 Ron Spellman, 7; Lt. Comdr. C. T. O'Neil, 10; 13, 15, 20–21, 26–27, 32–33, 40–41, 47, 48–49, 70–71, back cover; Petty Officer Jonathon R. Cilley, 23; PA1 Kurt Frederickson, 30; Seaman Sabrinna Elgammal, 34–35; Petty Officer 2nd Class Thomas M. Blue/Petty Officer Second Class Shawn Eggert, 37; PA2 Jennifer Johnson, 38; Petty Officer 3rd Class Melissa Hauck, 42; Petty Officer 3rd Class Erik Swanson, 44–45; Lt. C. T. O'Neil, 52; Tom Sperduto, 54–55; Petty Officer 2nd Class Christopher D. McLaughlin, 57; PAC Telfair H. Brown, 60–61; PA3 Walter Shinn, 62–63; Petty Officer 3rd Class Tara Molle, 65; Petty Officer Richard Brahm, 73.

Printed in Malaysia
1 3 5 6 4 2

CONTENTS

GUARDING
OUR NATION'S
SHORES AND SEAS

The United States Revenue Cutter Service, predecessor to the United States Coast Guard, was established on August 4, 1790, by President George Washington and the U.S. Congress. The service, which was part of the nation's Department of the Treasury, was in charge of collecting taxes from ships bearing cargoes of imported goods to the United States. Congress approved the construction of ten cutters—small armed sailing ships—that were to be operated and maintained by forty men. The Revenue Cutter Service became the U.S. Coast Guard 125 years later, in 1915.

The Revenue Cutter Service—or the Revenue Marine, as it was also called—was not formed as a military organization; however, it was assigned to military duty when a brief, undeclared war erupted between the United States and France in 1798. Congress immediately authorized President John Adams, and his successors, to place the Revenue Marine under the U.S. Navy in times of war and other national emergencies.

Coast Guard personnel attending Officer Candidate School stand in formation with weapons at their sides.

The Revenue Marine's military involvement continued in the following decades. It captured enemy vessels, patrolled the coasts, and blockaded ports. During the Mexican-American War (1846–1848), the Revenue Marine was involved in the blockade of Mexico. It participated in the Spanish-American War in the 1898 Battle of Manila Bay alongside the Navy.

During the nineteenth century the Revenue Marine was also performing a wide variety of peacetime tasks. In 1880, for example, the service launched the Bering Sea Patrol, which provided medical services to the Inuit, enforced the treaties protecting seals, transported oceanographic expeditions to their destinations, and rescued the crews of whaling ships that had been trapped in the ice.

In 1914 a multination convention met in London and established the International Ice Patrol. The U.S. Revenue Cutter Service was to provide ships and personnel for the patrol, and other countries were to provide financial support. The following January, President Woodrow Wilson signed into law a measure that joined the Revenue Cutter Service with the Life-Saving Service, a civilian rescue agency. At the suggestion of Commandant Ellsworth Price Bertholf, who headed the new service, the organization was named the United States Coast Guard (USCG).

After the nation entered World War I in 1917 the Coast Guard supervised the commercial and military traffic that sailed to and from the United States. Coast Guard cutters also served as escorts for troop and supply convoys making their way to Europe.

The Coast Guard's duties increased during the ensuing decades. In 1939 it incorporated the U.S. Lighthouse Service, which was responsible for operating and maintaining the nation's lighthouses. In 1946 the Bureau of Marine Inspection and Navigation was transferred from the Commerce Department to the Coast Guard.

During World War II the number of personnel in the Coast Guard increased from 10,000 to 171,000. Of that total, approximately 108,000 served in the regular Coast Guard, 51,000 served in the Coast Guard Reserve, and more than 11,000 served in the Coast Guard Women's Reserve, whose members are usually called the SPARs. Coast Guard personnel, under the jurisdiction of the U.S. Navy, worked on 351 vessels, ranging from troop transports to landing craft. The Coast Guard's ships—principally cutters and patrol boats—sailed as convoy escorts and submarine chasers. In addition, Coast Guard personnel served aboard 288 of the Army's Transportation Corps ships.

In the years since World War II, the Coast Guard has served the nation in many ways. Its icebreakers, for example, carve paths for freighters and passenger ships and patrol the North Atlantic and Pacific oceans. Its ships also patrol the nation's coastline to intercept vessels trying to bring immigrants to the United States illegally.

Though the Coast Guard uses lots of advanced technology, the lines and ropes on vessels still need to be tied manually. Seaman Storekeeper Kareem J. Patterson (*right*) secures a towing line to the bitt aboard a utility boat. Matt F. Delahunty (*left*), a cadet at the Coast Guard Academy, looks on.

In 1967 the Coast Guard was transferred from the Treasury Department to the Department of Transportation and then, in 2003, it was placed under the newly established Department of Homeland Security. Though it is the nation's smallest military force, the Coast Guard is a formidable organization. As of 2009 there were 42,000 active-duty enlisted personnel and officers, approximately 12 percent of whom were women. The regular Coast Guard is assisted by

8,000 members of the Coast Guard Reserve and 34,000 members of the Coast Guard Auxiliary.

This book is aimed primarily at young men and women who are thinking of joining the U.S. Coast Guard. One reader may feel it is his or her patriotic duty. Another might wish to serve to honor the memory of a loved one or friend killed or injured in action. One person may see the Coast Guard as a career. Another may see the Coast Guard as the first step on the road to a university degree or the source of the technical training needed for future civilian work. Still others may join for the oldest reason of all: the desire to meet new people and see faraway places.

Time spent in the Coast Guard, no matter how long, brings rewards. It provides training and a sense of discipline that are useful in civilian life. The academic and practical experience men and women receive in a variety of technical, administrative, and service areas are respected assets in both military and civilian careers. Former members of the military are increasingly sought by civilian employers.

Service with the U.S. Coast Guard has quite a lot to offer.

THE COAST GUARD'S

MISSION

THE U.S. COAST GUARD IS THE PRINCIPAL federal agency responsible for maritime safety, security, and stewardship. Its safety initiative entails saving lives and protecting property. The Coast Guard ensures the security of the nation by maintaining a maritime law enforcement system. It fulfills the stewardship initiative by managing the effective use of the nation's inland, coastal, and ocean waters, with an emphasis on maintaining resources for the future.

According to these initiatives, the Coast Guard has three basic responsibilities: to protect the public, to protect the environment, and to protect the nation's economic and security interests in any ocean, coastal region, port, or inland waterway where they are threatened. The Coast

Coast Guard Station New York conducts search-and-rescue missions and provides security to New York waterways. Here, Petty Officer 3rd Class Valerie Thrall mans the machine gun on a patrol craft in New York Harbor.

Guard separates its duties into five mission areas: maritime safety, maritime mobility, maritime security, national defense, and the protection of natural resources. In addition, since September 11, 2001, the Coast Guard has been a component of the nation's heightened security initiative.

MARITIME SAFETY

The Coast Guard is responsible for keeping U.S. waters safe for vessels and their passengers. Coast Guard personnel investigate the cause of accidents of American and foreign ships in U.S. waters; respond to oil spills; conduct inspections of passenger, tanker, cargo, and pleasure craft; carry out surface and air search-and-rescue operations in American and international waters; participate in the International Ice Patrol; and work on safety measures to prevent accidental damage to vessels and port facilities. Inspection of the safety features required on recreational craft—flotation devices, radios, and distress signaling equipment—is also a duty of the Coast Guard.

MARITIME MOBILITY

Maintaining and improving maritime mobility—the flow of goods and passengers through U.S. waters and selected foreign waters—is one of the principal tasks of Coast Guard personnel. They are responsible for installing and maintaining the nation's navigational and visual aids, which include radio navigation systems, buoys, and daymarks. (A daymark is a navigational aid, such as a tower, distinctively marked for visibility during daylight hours.)

MARITIME SECURITY

Maritime security entails protecting the United States from illegal activities, including illicit drug trade and illegal immigration, both of which pose major challenges for the Coast Guard. The Coast Guard also monitors prohibited fishing activities and other violations of federal law on navigable waters.

During a Coast Guard operation in the Bahamas, personnel found $80 million in cocaine aboard a 200-foot (61-m) motor vessel. Florida-based Coast Guard aircrewmen flew in to help off-load the seized cocaine.

Every year thousands of foreigners attempt to enter the United States without the legal clearance to do so. It is the Coast Guard's duty to intercept those who attempt to enter the country or its territories by sea. Most of those who try to enter by sea come from the island nations in the Caribbean (Cuba, Jamaica, Haiti, and the Dominican Republic) and the northern shores of South America. If the service intercepts these migrants before they manage to come ashore in the United States, they can be turned around quickly. According to Coast Guard statistics, on an average day, the Coast Guard and Coast Guard Reserve stop twenty-six illegal migrants from entering the United States. That adds up to nearly 9,500 people a year. Other U.S. agencies—the Navy, Customs and Border Protection (CBP), and Immigration and Customs Enforcement (ICE)—also patrol U.S. coastal waters. Any other vessel at sea (for instance, a private yacht or cruise liner) that intercepts migrants must turn them over to the Coast Guard, which then holds them until the U.S. Citizenship and Immigration Services (USCIS) determines whether they should be returned home or granted amnesty.

Drug smuggling has been a problem for the Coast Guard since the 1870s, when Chinese immigrants began smuggling opium into California aboard merchant and passenger ships. In the decades since, drug smuggling has grown to include marijuana, cocaine, and heroin, among

NEVER A DULL MOMENT

Since it was first established, one of the Coast Guard's primary concerns has been maritime safety and security. As a result, Coast Guard personnel are quite busy.

On an average day the U.S. Coast Guard:
- Saves 15 lives
- Assists 114 people in distress
- Protects $4.9 million in property
- Conducts 82 search-and-rescue cases
- Seizes $12.4 million worth of illegal drugs
- Conducts 122 security boardings and 202 law enforcement boardings
- Stops 26 illegal immigrants from entering the United States

many other substances. The Coast Guard, with the help of the Navy, federal and state agencies, and neighboring countries, monitors more than 6 million square miles (15.5 million square kilometers) of ocean bordering the United States. Between 1997 and early 2008, for example, Coast Guard crews seized more than 400 tons (364 metric tons) of cocaine and over 160 tons (145 mt) of marijuana.

NATIONAL DEFENSE

The Coast Guard protects the nation's coasts, ports, and inland waterways from threats from both foreign and domestic forces. Since September 11, 2001, there has been an understandably greater emphasis placed on protecting the nation from terrorist attacks.

In the wake of the attacks, the federal government reorganized its management of the nation's defense and formally established the Department of Homeland Security in November 2002. The Coast Guard, as watchdog of the nation's ships, coasts, and waters, refocused its efforts and developed new tools to accommodate the higher level of national security. To meet the demands, the Coast Guard mobilized 2,000 reservists to patrol the more than 360 ports and 95,000 miles of coastline for which the service is responsible. The Coast Guard has eleven Homeland Security mission-programs that have been formalized in legislation. Each supports the Coast Guard's safety, security, and stewardship initiatives.

1. Aids to Navigation
2. Defense Readiness
3. Drug Interdiction
4. Ice Operations
5. Living Marine Resources
6. Marine Environmental Protection
7. Marine Safety
8. Migrant Interdiction
9. Ports, Waterways, and Coastal Security
10. Search and Rescue
11. Other Law Enforcement

PROTECTION OF NATURAL RESOURCES

The Coast Guard is responsible for protecting the environment from damage caused by maritime traffic, recreational boating, and commercial and recreational fishing. A major part of the job concerns problems related to ocean liners, merchant ships, and oil tankers. Whenever an accident involves a contaminant spill, for example, the Coast Guard is in charge of stopping the spread of the hazardous material and preventing it from coming ashore. The Coast Guard then works with the police, the harbor authorities, and the ship's

It is important that the Coast Guard responds quickly to oil spills to minimize contamination. Here, cleanup crewmembers remove oil-absorbent bags from the Mississippi River. The bags had been put in place to soak up oil after a spill.

officers and owners in assessing the amount and type of damage.

The Coast Guard's National Response Center (NRC) is one of the service's most important tools. The center collects and reports data relating to incidents in which oil, chemicals, and biological, radiological, or disease-causing materials are spilled into the waters around the United States and its territories. After a spill has occurred, the information gathered allows the cleanup to proceed swiftly and efficiently. In addition, the NRC gathers and distributes reports of terrorist activities and other breaches of maritime security.

The captain of a vessel entering U.S. territorial waters must provide the Coast Guard with the ship's name and a list of its cargo, the names and passport data of all crew members, information on the ship's owners and agents, and a list of the ports recently visited.

This information is kept on file by U.S. Naval Intelligence and by officials at ports throughout the nation. The authorities at the port of arrival use the information to decide whether the ship needs to be inspected for safety or security. Incoming vessels must be inspected by the Coast Guard every six months.

SEA, AIR, AND LAND

To carry out missions successfully and fulfill its responsibilities, the Coast Guard is equipped with cutters, boats, and aircraft, as well weapons, wheeled vehicles, and communications systems. All members of the U.S. Coast Guard and the Coast Guard Reserve must become acquainted with the equipment, weapons, and technology associated with their rating.

CUTTERS

As of early 2009 the Coast Guard had more than 250 cutters at its disposal, including 12 high endurance cutters, 28 medium endurance cutters, 118 patrol boats, 4 icebreakers, one sail training ship, one training and support tender, 35 seagoing and coastal buoy tenders, 31 inland and river tenders, and 20 tugboats. All ships that are classified as cutters must measure at least 65 feet (19.8 meters) in length, carry a permanently assigned crew, and have accommodations for extra crew as required.

The *Boutwell*, a 378-foot (115-m) high endurance cutter, made its first international stop in Shanghai, China, as part of the North Pacific Coast Guard Forum. The forum aims to improve maritime safety and security in the northern Pacific.

HIGH ENDURANCE CUTTERS The Coast Guard's high endurance cutters are rugged ships powered by four engines (two diesels and two gas turbines) for high-speed operation. They are patrol vessels built for long-range duties on the open ocean.

With a length of 378 feet (115.2 m) and a displacement of 3,250 tons (2,948 mt), these *Hamilton*-class cutters are the second-largest ships constructed for the Coast Guard (a ship's class is named after the first vessel of its design). Each has a range of 14,000 miles (22,500 km) and comes equipped with a helicopter flight deck and a retractable hangar.

In August 2008 the first national security cutter, the 418-foot (127-m) *Bertholf*, was commissioned. It is the first of eight planned ships in the new *Legend* class that will replace the *Hamilton*-class cutters.

MEDIUM ENDURANCE CUTTERS Medium endurance cutters are, as the name implies, slightly less rugged than their high endurance companions. There are five classes of medium endurance cutters, three of which—the *Acushnet,* the *Storis,* and the *Edenton*—have just one ship each. All remaining cutters are members of either *Bear*-class or *Reliance*-class ships.

Bear- and *Reliance*-class cutters are powered by two diesel engines. *Bear*-class cutters are considerably larger, however; each is 270 feet (82.3 m) long, weighs 1,780 tons (1,615 mt) fully loaded, and carries a crew of one hundred. A *Reliance*-class cutter is 210 feet (64 m) long, weighs 1,050 tons (955 mt) fully loaded and carries a sixty-two-member crew.

The thirteen ships in the *Bear* class are multipurpose vessels. They were designed for fourteen-day patrols, but are commonly at sea in the Caribbean for up to ninety-day stints in efforts to curb illegal immigration.

The fourteen *Reliance*-class cutters are used for law-enforcement duties and search-and-rescue missions. These ships have long been the Coast Guard's workhorses, though they are not as fast as newly designed vessels.

ICEBREAKERS

The Coast Guard operates and maintains four icebreakers: the *Healy*, the *Mackinaw*, the *Polar Star*, and the *Polar Sea*. The ships range from 16,400 tons (14,910 mt) and 420 feet (128 m) long to 3,394 tons (3085.5 mt) and 240 feet (73 m) long.

The *Healy* was launched in 1999. It is powered by four diesel engines, carries a crew of sixty-three, and can break through 4.5 feet (1.4 m) of ice at 3 knots (5.5 km/hour). (Speed at sea is measured in knots, or nautical miles per hour. One nautical mile equals 1.15 standard miles.) The ship is equipped with a landing pad, hangar, and two Dolphin helicopters that survey distant ice problems. With 4,200 square feet (390 m^2) of laboratory space and accommodations for as many as fifty scientists, the *Healy* can engage in a wide variety of oceanic studies and experiments.

The *Mackinaw*, launched in 2005, is powered by three diesel engines. The ship's main job is to keep shipping lanes open on the Great Lakes; in ice-free months it serves as a buoy tender, so it has a dual classification.

The icebreaker *Polar Star* plows a channel through frozen Antarctic waters.

The *Polar Star* and *Polar Sea* are both capable of handling a wide variety of scientific missions and can accommodate fifty and thirty-five scientists, respectively. With six diesel engines and three gas turbines each, the ships can carve through 6 feet (1.83 m) of ice at 3 knots (5.6 km/h).

BOATS

The Coast Guard classifies its 1,660 vessels measuring less than 65 feet (19.8 m) as boats. The smaller size enables boats to work close to shore and along inland waterways. The Coast Guard operates armed boats and pursuit boats, motor lifeboats, utility rescue boats, shipboard boats, aids-to-navigation boats, flood-relief punts, ice-rescue skiffs, and service, support, and training boats.

As of 2009 the only vessel in the armed and pursuit boat category was the transportable port security boat. The forty-four boats of this type are mainly used to provide security in ports that serve as support areas and points of embarkation and debarkation for U.S. forces. The 25-foot-long (7.6 m) security boat is well known and respected for its maneuverability, versatility, and durability.

AIRCRAFT

The Coast Guard operates approximately 200 fixed-wing and rotary aircraft. The HU-25A Guardian (Falcon) medium-range surveillance jet and the HC-130 Hercules long-range surveillance plane and cargo carrier are the two types of fixed-wing aircraft used by the service. The rotary aircraft include the HH-60J Jayhawk medium-range helicopter, the MH-68A Stingray interdiction helicopter, and the HH-65C Dolphin short-range recovery helicopter.

The Coast Guard's helicopters are used in search-and-rescue missions, law enforcement, illegal drug interdiction, illegal alien interdiction, transportation of passengers and supplies, marine environmental protection, ice operations, and military readiness.

THE COAST GUARD RACING STRIPE

In 1964, President John F. Kennedy had an industrial design firm create visual identification symbols for U.S government agencies and departments. The firm, Raymond Loewy/William Snaith, Inc., suggested the Coast Guard adopt something simple that was easily distinguishable from marks of other agencies.

The firm designed a trio of bars set an angle of 64 degrees: a narrow blue stripe, a narrow white stripe, and a wide red stripe overlaid with the Coast Guard emblem.

By April 6, 1967, three years after work on the design began, the racing stripe appeared on all Coast Guard vessels. The design became so highly regarded that it was adopted by the Canadian Coast Guard, the Indian Coast Guard, the Italian Guardia Costiera, and the Australian Customs Service. The stripe later even came to adorn the Coast Guard's letterhead, website, and offical publications.

Three Coast Guard MH-60 Jayhawk helicopters fly in formation over Kodiak Island, Alaska.

WEAPONS, VEHICLES, AND COMMUNICATIONS SYSTEMS

For tasks and missions that require ground transportation, the Coast Guard has many kinds of vehicles, including trucks, cars, and ambulances. In addition, a service as large and complex as the Coast Guard requires a variety of weapons, both large and small, to best carry out its duties. While on patrol, personnel are armed with pistols. Many men and women with the Coast Guard are also trained to use the M16A rifle, the main personal weapon used by the rest of the military branches, and a police magnum riot shotgun. Many Coast Guard vessels and aircraft are equipped with machine guns, so personnel on those crafts are instructed in proper machine-gun handling and maintenance. The Coast Guard also has an up-to-date communications system with provision for secure transmission and safeguards against hostile interference. Coast Guard personnel are trained in the operation and maintenance of this system.

CHOOSING A
CAREER

THERE ARE MANY JOB OPPORTUNITIES IN the Coast Guard, and all are integral to the service's efficiency and success. The men and women with the Coast Guard must keep the service's boats and aircraft in operational order and must maintain and monitor its surveillance and data-collecting systems.

The jobs assigned to enlisted personnel are called ratings, a term that is also used by the Navy. In the Army and Marine Corps the equivalent term is military occupational specialties, and in the Air Force it is specialty codes.

The training of Coast Guard personnel begins at the recruit's first duty station and entails classroom work and on-the-job training. Highly technical ratings require further classroom and practical training at a Coast Guard class A school

Coastguardsmen aboard the cutter *Juniper* bring an oil skimmer on board during an oil spill exercise in Narragansett Bay. The skimmer, which must be operated in calm water, has a floating storage unit that can hold 13,200 gallons (50 kiloliters) of oil.

(advanced training is offered at class B and C schools). Any member of the Coast Guard who meets the academic and physical admissions standards may apply to a class A school.

Many of the ratings listed here are available to members of both the Coast Guard and the Coast Guard Reserve. Ratings open to enlisted personnel are divided into four categories: Deck and Ordnance, Hull and Engineering, Aviation, and Administrative and Scientific.

DECK AND ORDNANCE GROUP

Jobs relating to the operation of Coast Guard vessels—navigation, deck supervision, and deck maintenance—fall into the Deck and Ordnance category. Boatswain's mates have the widest range of responsibilities. Someone with this rating may supervise the deck force, operate cargo-loading winches, navigate the vessel, or stand security

In 2008 the Coast Guard began installing Vega, a new navigational system that will eventually replace existing shipboard electronic navigation software. Here, Seaman Casey Todd uses Vega aboard the cutter *Pendant*.

watch. A gunner's mate works with weapons and also trains other Coast Guard personnel in the proper handling of weapons and ammunition. An operations specialist is in charge of tactical command information and must operate the tactical computer systems for law enforcement operations and search-and-rescue missions. An intelligence specialist collects, analyzes, processes, and disseminates data related to Coast Guard missions. The intelligence rating was recently added to maintain high levels of homeland security.

HULL AND ENGINEERING GROUP

Personnel with ratings in the Hull and Engineering category are responsible for the upkeep and operation of Coast Guard vessels. A damage controlman on a cutter, for example, makes sure the vessel is watertight and that the onboard emergency equipment is functional. The Coast Guard uses sophisticated electrical and electronic equipment; electrician's mates and electronics technicians are responsible for its installation, maintenance, repair, and management. The machinery technician rating is one held by a large number of Coast Guard personnel. These men and women are trained to operate and maintain every piece of machinery aboard a Coast Guard vessel or at a shore station. The Hull and Engineering group also includes information system technicians, who establish and maintain telephone and computer systems and those systems' infrastructure; at sea they are also responsible for the tactical command systems.

With so many vessels, planes, and vehicles, the Coast Guard needs many mechanical specialists to keep everything in working order. Fireman Sasha Baker works on the main engine of the cutter *Eagle*.

AVIATION GROUP

All ratings related to the maintenance and operation of Coast Guard aircraft (except for the rating of pilot) are included in the Aviation category. Aviation maintenance technicians inspect, service, maintain, and repair all nonelectronic parts of Coast Guard aircraft. Their counterparts, avionics electrical technicians, are responsible for the rest: communications, navigation, collision-avoidance, and target-acquisition systems. This category also includes aviation survival technicians; swimmers who work as members of rescue

In 2005, Lieutenant Junior Grade Jeanine Menze became the Coast Guard's first African-American female aviator. Here she is at the controls of a C-130 Hercules.

WOMEN IN THE COAST GUARD

Women have been fulfilling maritime safety duties since the 1830s, when they worked as lighthouse keepers for the U.S. Lighthouse Service (in 1939 this service became part of the U.S. Coast Guard). Lighthouse service was one of the first nonclerical government jobs open to women, though many actually inherited the positions from their husbands or fathers.

The Coast Guard Women's Reserve was formed in 1942 and placed under the command of Captain Dorothy C. Stratton, the former dean of women at Purdue University. During World War II more than 11,000 women served with the Coast Guard Women's Reserve. They were nicknamed SPARs, a moniker derived from the Coast Guard's motto, *Semper Paratus* ("always ready"). SPARs worked as clerical and medical personnel, as did women serving with the other branches of the military.

In 1948 Congress passed the Women's Armed Services Integration Act, a measure that codified the position of women in the military. Like men, women could hold regular military ranks with duties and privileges appropriate to each rank. Regulations for men and women continued to be different, however, and women continued to be restricted from combat duty.

Though the SPARs program was discontinued after World War II, it was revived in 1950 and renamed the Women's Reserve of the U.S. Coast Guard. In 1973 new federal legislation further reduced sex-based distinctions within the Coast Guard and integrated women into active duty; while no women were assigned to actual combat duty, they were allowed to serve in combat areas. That same year the first women were admitted to Officer's Candidate School. Women in the Coast Guard reached another milestone in 1975 when they were assigned to flight training. In 1976 the Coast Guard Academy became the first of the military academies to admit female students, and in 1977 a Coast Guard ship with some female crew members set out to sea. Finally, in 1978 all career officer fields and enlisted ratings in the Coast Guard were opened to female personnel.

Avionics electrical technicians, such as Petty Officer 3rd Class Gene Starling, are responsible for conducting pre-flight checks of Coast Guard aircraft to check that electrical flight instruments are functioning properly.

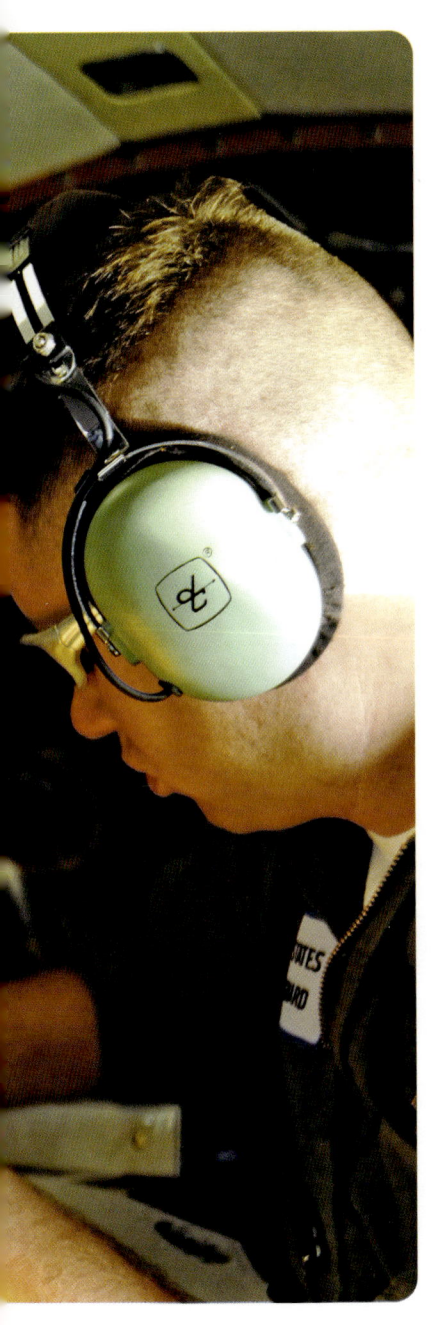

teams (for accidents involving helicopters or ships) and emergency medical technicians hold Aviation group ratings.

ADMINISTRATIVE AND SCIENTIFIC GROUP

Personnel in the Administrative and Scientific group provide vital support services for the Coast Guard's primary mission. Administrative ratings are concerned with food, shelter, medical services, and all other goods and services that Coast Guard personnel need. A food services specialist has culinary, accounting, and management training to provide meals and maintain dining facilities. Storekeepers procure and distribute clothing, spare parts, and all other supplies to Coast Guard personnel. Health services technicians provide routine and emergency health care ashore and at sea.

Petty officers 1st class Luke Potter and Brian Atkison are members of the Pacific Strike Team, which is a world-recognized authority in the preparation for and response to hazardous substances and weapons of mass destruction, among other emergencies. Potter, a marine science technician, and Atkison, an electrician's mate, sample the contents of a drum while wearing protective suits.

Public affairs specialists communicate with the media and transmit official Coast Guard policies and positions.

Scientific ratings are largely concerned with the protection of natural resources. Marine science technicians, for example, respond to oil and chemical spills and inspect waterfront facilities. They also monitor the pollution levels and species populations of U.S. waters and inspect vessels and facilities to make sure they are in compliance with U.S. laws. Marine science technician assignments include domestic vessel examination, port state control, harbor patrol, or maritime security.

THREE

COAST GUARD
SERVICE

MEN AND WOMEN WHO ENLIST IN THE U.S. Coast Guard can serve in any one of four ways: as active-duty Coast Guard personnel, as members of the Coast Guard Reserve, as members of the Coast Guard Auxiliary, or as cadets at the Coast Guard Academy in New London, Connecticut. Active-duty and Reserve personnel and academy applicants must meet certain requirements:

- They must be a U.S. citizen or meet noncitizen requirements.
- They must be between the ages of seventeen and thirty-four; those who are seventeen need parental consent.
- They must be high school graduates or have a high school equivalency diploma.
- They must have no more than two dependents.

Crewmembers onboard the *Sherman* duck as they move away from an H-65 Dolphin after tying the helicopter down to the cutter's deck.

Enlistees must also pass urinalysis tests for drug and alcohol abuse and must meet a variety of legal and medical standards.

ACTIVE DUTY IN THE COAST GUARD

For those on active service, the Coast Guard is a full-time job. An enlistee signs up for a four- or six-year period of service and begins his or her Coast Guard career as a seaman recruit.

After successfully completing basic training, most recruits are assigned to a ship or to a shore station. In this early period of enlistment, their assignments tend to be unglamorous: they tend to kitchen duties, swab decks and barrack floors, and perform other daily support tasks. However, specialized training in a rating also begins at a recruit's first duty station.

There are promotion opportunities for men and women who exhibit competence and wish to pursue a career with the Coast Guard. With higher rank comes greater responsibilities and new opportunities to develop leadership and other professional skills. Salary increases both annually and with each promotion. Within the enlisted ranks someone might rise to become a chief petty officer; an enlisted man or woman with exceptional leadership skills can apply to become a warrant officer. Those who wish to pursue a career as a commissioned officer in the Coast Guard may apply for admission to Officer Candidate School, where advanced leadership training is provided. Although officers have specialties as well, their principal task is leadership, since they oversee a wide range of activities not related to their specialty.

COAST GUARD RESERVE

The Coast Guard Reserve was established by Congress in 1939. It was originally an organization of civilian boat owners who volunteered to assist the Coast Guard in a variety of activities. They promoted general water safety, inspected docking facilities for safety and improvement, and gave advice and assistance to boating groups.

The Coast Guard and Coast Guard Reserve often team up for patrol duty during large events, such as Canal Day in Chesapeake City, Maryland. The annual event attracts hundreds of boats and thousands of visitors.

In 1941 Congress restructured the Coast Guard Reserve into two separate groups: the Coast Guard Reserve and the Coast Guard Auxiliary. At the end of World War II (1945), the Reserve and the Auxiliary became two entirely separate organizations.

As of 2009 the Coast Guard Reserve was a force of 8,000 officers and enlisted personnel. Reservists are trained to perform the same jobs as active-duty members; however, they serve one weekend each month and a two-week period of full-time service each year.

Members of the Reserve may be called to active duty in the event of a local or national emergency. According to federal law, reservists can serve a maximum of two years on active duty. The law also requires the reservist's civilian employer to reinstate a returning reservist to the job he or she held or to provide an equivalent position. The reservist must have notified his or her employer of the call to active duty and must return immediately to work.

Men and women who join the Coast Guard Reserve are assigned to duty with a unit located close to where they live. Reservists are able to continue working or attending school and lead normal civilian lives except for the required periods of duty.

COAST GUARD AUXILIARY

The Coast Guard Auxiliary is a volunteer organization whose members spend countless hours assisting the

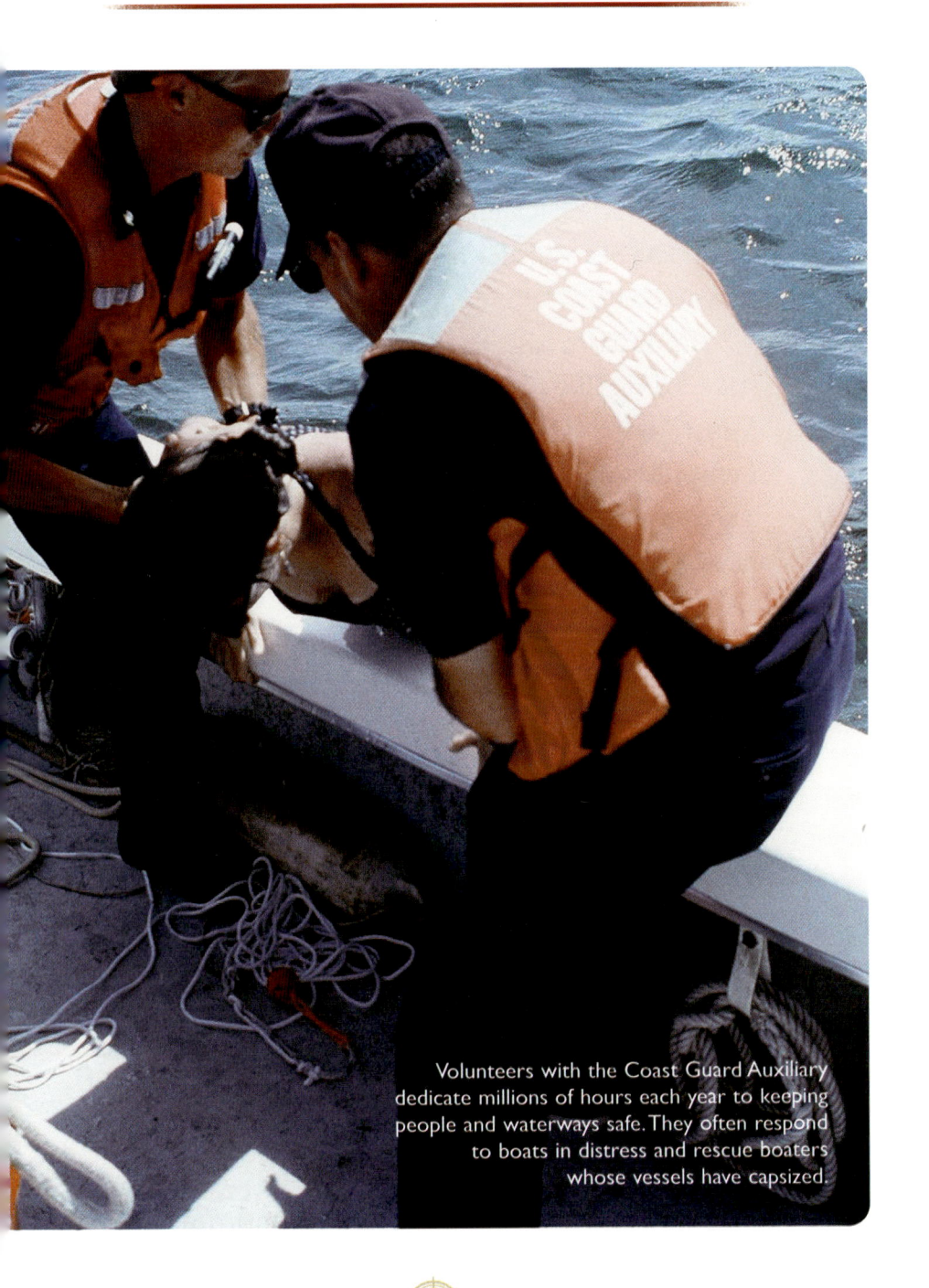

Volunteers with the Coast Guard Auxiliary dedicate millions of hours each year to keeping people and waterways safe. They often respond to boats in distress and rescue boaters whose vessels have capsized.

Coast Guard each year. Members participate in search-and-rescue operations, safety checks of civilian boats and docking facilities, patrols of regatta and marina events, and course instruction for amateur sailors. All areas of work are open to Auxiliary members except military operations and law enforcement.

The Auxiliary has 34,000 members throughout the fifty states, Puerto Rico, the Virgin Islands, Guam, the Northern Mariana Islands, and American Samoa. Though auxiliarists work with or aboard private boats, they are not required to own a boat to join. The Coast Guard does stipulate, however, that members have a desire to serve the public on or around water.

U.S. COAST GUARD ACADEMY

The U.S. Coast Guard Academy (USCGA) is located in New London, Connecticut. With a student population of approximately 1,000 men and women (women make up almost 30 percent of the student body), it is the smallest of the nation's leading military schools.

The academy was established in 1876 in New Bedford, Massachusetts, as the School of Instruction of the Revenue Cutter Service. When the Revenue Cutter Service and the Life-Saving Service were united as the U.S. Coast Guard in 1915, the school became the Coast Guard Academy; it was relocated to New London in 1932.

A Coast Guard Academy applicant must be between seventeen and twenty-two years of age, unmarried, and a

AN ACADEMY OPPORTUNITY FOR MINORITY STUDENTS

The Coast Guard Academy offers several programs for minority applicants interested in specific areas of study. The Minority Introduction to Engineering (MITE), for example, is a six-day program conducted twice each July at the Coast Guard Academy. The highly selective program provides successful minority applicants with an introduction to career opportunities provided by the Coast Guard in engineering and related fields.

To apply for the program a student must be a U.S. citizen of minority heritage with an interest in and an aptitude for engineering. Two years of high school mathematics and strong scores on such standardized achievement examinations as the PSAT or ACT are required. Applicants are also expected to be good students and to meet the academy's medical and physical-fitness standards.

Coast Guard Academy cadets study a map on the deck of the *Eagle*. The cadets worked aboard the cutter alongside thirty-eight crewmembers to gain hands-on experience.

U.S. citizen. In addition, prospective students must pass a military physical examination and meet several academic requirements, among them having a high school diploma and having taken four units each of high school English and mathematics. Students accepted to the academy receive full government scholarships for tuition and the costs of books, uniforms, room and board, and medical and dental care, as well as a monthly salary. Graduates earn bachelor of science (BS) degrees and are commissioned ensigns in the Coast Guard. They must fulfill a five-year active-duty commitment after graduation.

Unlike the other military academies, the Coast Guard Academy does not require applicants to be nominated by a member of Congress or other government official. Rather, it accepts students solely on the basis of their academic achievements and personal merits.

Life as an academy cadet begins with Swab Summer. An experience that is very similar to boot camp, Swab Summer is a seven-week period of intense physical, military, academic, and professional training that takes place before the first academic semester begins. Cadets spend subsequent summers in professional training.

The Coast Guard Academy offers programs in eight majors: civil engineering, mechanical engineering, electrical engineering, naval architecture and marine engineering, marine and environmental sciences, operations research and computer analysis, government, and management.

FOUR

ENLISTMENT
AND TRAINING

ANY DECISION THAT WILL INVOLVE FOUR or more years of a person's life is a big one. The decision to join the U.S. Coast Guard is no exception. Some who make the choice are looking for a career with the Coast Guard, while others want to acquire skills for civilian use or simply want to do something that promises adventure and excitement. It is advisable to talk with family, friends, and even a favorite teacher before reaching a final decision. Whatever the motive for joining the Coast Guard, the first step is enlisting.

ENLISTMENT

Enlistment begins at a local Coast Guard recruiting station, where a recruiter will provide an introduction to life in the Coast Guard and answer a prospective enlistee's questions. A recruiter can

Physical conditioning is a major part of basic training in the Coast Guard. Seaman recruits at the Coast Guard Training Center do push-ups on the beach in Cape May, New Jersey.

also help determine whether the active-duty Coast Guard or the Coast Guard Reserve best suits an enlistee's goals.

New recruits undergo a military physical examination, receive a copy of the *Helmsman* (the Coast Guard's training guidebook), and take the Armed Services Vocational Aptitude Battery (ASVAB). The ASVAB is a series of multiple-choice tests; the subjects include general science, arithmetic reasoning, electronics, and mechanical comprehension. The ASVAB is not an intelligence (IQ) or academic test; its purpose is to gain information about an enlistee's aptitudes to determine which Coast Guard jobs will utilize his or her strengths.

The Coast Guard also offers a Delayed Entry Program (DEP) that allows an enlistee to delay reporting for duty for as long as a year. This program is useful if an enlistee wants to complete school before entering the service or if he or she has a personal or business matter to reconcile. Even though their lives as civilians continue, the men and women who take advantage of the program are still in the Coast Guard and must report for duty at the agreed-upon time.

BOOT CAMP

After completing all the required testing, recruits report for boot camp, an eight-week-long training period at the U.S. Coast Guard Training Center in Cape May, New Jersey. Boot camp introduces recruits to Coast Guard life and to military protocol; enlistees are trained in first aid, seamanship, weapons handling, and the techniques of water survival. A large part of the physical training involves swimming.

Men and women train together at boot camp but are housed separately. Recruits are divided into companies of fifty to sixty; each company is assigned to a company commander (CC) who will help the recruits through all their training.

WEEK ONE

During the first week recruits are introduced to daily physical exercise, company drills, and living-quarters maintenance, activities that will continue for the rest of the training period. Recruits also attend a class on the Uniform Code of Military Justice to learn about punishable offenses in the service.

A shipboard fire is a very dangerous situation, so all Coast Guard recruits undergo firefighting training. They practice using the hoses (*shown*) before training in full fire protection gear, which they wear during the final firefighting test.

WEEK TWO

During the second week classroom work includes instruction in the rights and duties of Coast Guard personnel, in ratings (pay grades) and ranks, in military protocol (for example, how to address other military personnel), and in stress management. Recruits also take what is called a survival float test, which checks their ability to stay afloat in the water.

WEEK THREE

In the third week recruits become acquainted with the 9 mm handgun, the basic weapon used in the Coast Guard. In the classroom they learn more about pay and allowances, the Montgomery GI Bill, deck seamanship, deckhand protective equipment, and the missions, traditions, and code of conduct of the Coast Guard.

WEEK FOUR

In the fourth week recruits participate in target practice with their handguns. Classroom activities include instruction in a wide range of other matters: leave and liberty (that is, extended and brief vacations), rating and nonrating duties (job-specific and general duties), insignia of rank and service, and vessels and aircraft.

In addition, two important tests are given at the end of week four to mark the midpoint of boot camp. The first, a written examination, checks mastery of all the classroom material covered in the first four weeks. If a recruit does not pass the exam, he or she is allowed one retest. The second test is the physical training (PT) test. Those who do not pass must train for an extra hour each morning to improve their physical fitness. Recruits who fail to complete all the PT requirements by week seven are sent to another company for further training.

At the end of the fourth week, recruits fill out an assignment data card (ADC), nicknamed the "dream sheet." On the cards recruits list places where they would prefer being stationed and the work they would like to do.

WEEK FIVE

During the fifth week recruits learn about deck maintenance and painting, boat crew and buoyancy, personal floatation devices, emergency and survival equipment, fire terminology, flags and pennants, and personal finance. There are also emergency drills.

WEEK SIX

Training in week six focuses on fire protection, prevention, and fighting. Recruits are instructed in fire-extinguishing methods, hose-handling techniques, and standing watch. Career counseling is also a part of the sixth week.

WEEK SEVEN

The emphasis of week seven is on the final examination, a cumulative review of basic-training material. Recruits who did not pass the PT test in week four are given another chance. A recruit must pass both the written examination and the PT test to graduate and become an official member of the Coast Guard.

WEEK EIGHT

Boot camp concludes with a formal graduation ceremony in which honor ribbons are awarded to the top 3 percent of the graduating company on the basis of written tests and instructor evaluations. Individuals who excel in academics, leadership, seamanship, manual-of-arms (handling of firearms) proficiency, marksmanship, and physical fitness also receive awards, as do those judged best shipmate.

A student repairs a motor as part of his training to be a machinery technician in the A school at the Reserve Training Center in Yorktown, Virginia. The machinery technician rating is the largest in the Coast Guard. In order to graduate from A school, students must be competent in all areas of machinery operation and maintenance. Once on duty, they will work on engines, ventilation systems, hydraulics, and basic electrical work.

CAREERS IN THE U.S. COAST GUARD

READY TO SERVE

After boot camp, recruits are assigned to one of four areas: Operational Afloat, Operational Ashore, Operations Support, or General Support. These areas cover all duty stations, both on land and sea, and both operational and support duties. Most recruits are placed in Operational Afloat because it is the Coast Guard's top priority. These new members of the Coast Guard are watched closely and judged on their abilities and enthusiasm. During this first assignment new personnel get to put into practice their boot camp training and learn firsthand about the workings of a ship. Those who perform well have a better chance of being placed in the rating of their choice.

Recruits also begin work in a career field at their first duty station. The Coast Guard uses an apprentice system to provide job training to new members; every boot camp graduate works alongside an experienced seaman, who provides hands-on training and personal coaching. Those men and women who wish to get job training in highly specialized fields may attend a class A school, which provides classroom and practical learning

Lieutenant Junior Grade Sarah Morin and Petty Officer 3rd Class Michael Hernon swim through icy Alaskan waters as part of a five-day survival training course. The Coast Guard officers wear insulated suits to prevent hypothermia.

opportunities. Any member of the Coast Guard who meets the academic and physical admissions standards may apply to a class A school.

ENLISTED RANKS AND PAY GRADES

The men and women in the U.S. Coast Guard, like those in the other branches of the armed forces, serve in one of three categories of rank: as enlisted personnel, as warrant officers, or as commissioned officers. A rank is a title, and a pay grade is an alphanumeric designation. The nine Coast Guard pay grades for enlisted personnel begin with the letter E.

Seaman Recruit, Seaman Apprentice, and Seaman, the lowest ranks, correspond to pay grades E-1, E-2, and E-3. Once a recruit graduates basic training, he or she is promoted to seaman apprentice and reports to his or her first unit to begin specialized job training.

Beginning with the pay grade E-4, Petty Officer Third Class, Coast Guard personnel are considered noncommissioned officers (NCOs). Coast Guard NCOs, as in the other services, are enlisted personnel who have been given command responsibilities. A commissioned officer usually has at least a college degree and has undergone special training; he or she delegates responsibility to NCOs. To become a petty officer, one must have either graduated from a specific rating's class A school or completed the rating's on-the-job training program. Subsequent promotions—to Petty

Officer Second Class (E-5), Petty Officer First Class (E-6), and Chief Petty Officer (E-7)—may follow.

Senior Chief Petty Officer (E-8) and Master Chief Petty Officer (E-9) are the two highest ranks and pay grades most enlisted personnel achieve. The few who have achieved these ranks have demonstrated expertise in their rating, have amassed significant experience, and have shown themselves able to handle the administrative duties required of senior NCOs. Within the E-9 pay grade are two special ranks:

Machinery Technician John Kovacevich is promoted to Petty Officer 1st Class in a ceremony onboard the *Eagle*. Petty Officer 1st Class Brian Seibert, pins insignia, nicknamed "crows," onto Kovacevich's collar.

COAST GUARD RANK INSIGNIA

ENLISTED RANKS

Coast Guard personnel wear their insignia indicating rank on the sleeves of their uniforms. In the Coast Guard, patterns of stripes, chevron, stars, and an eagle make up each enlisted rank insignia.

Seaman Recruit (SR)

Seaman Apprentice (SA)

Seaman (SN)

Petty Officer Third Class (PO3)

Petty Officer Second Class (PO2)

Petty Officer First Class (PO1)

Chief Petty Officer (CPO)

Senior Chief Petty Officer (SCPO)

Master Chief Petty Officer (MCPO)

Command Master Chief Petty Officer (CMCPO)

Master Chief Petty Officer of the Coast Guard (MCPO-CG)

OFFICERS

Rank insignia for commissioned officers in the Coast Guard are similar to those used in the Navy. Silver and gold bars and leaves, an eagle, and silver stars indicate the ranks.

 Ensign (ENS)

 Rear Admiral Upper Half (RADM)(U)

 Lieutenant Junior Grade (LTJG)

 Vice Admiral (VADM)

 Lieutenant (LT)

 Admiral (ADM)

 Lieutenant Commander (LCDR)

 Fleet Admiral (FADM)

 Commander (CDR)

 Chief Warrant Officer 2 (CWO2)

 Captain (CAPT)

 Chief Warrant Officer 3 (CWO3)

 Chief Warrant Officer 4 (CWO4)

 Rear Admiral Lower Half (RADM)(L)

Command Master Chief Petty Officer and Master Chief Petty Officer of the Coast Guard. The former rank may be held by the senior enlisted member of a major Coast Guard command. The latter rank, held by only one individual at a given time, is awarded to the senior enlisted adviser to the commandant of the Coast Guard.

COAST GUARD OFFICERS

Most commissioned Coast Guard officers are graduates of the Coast Guard's Officer Candidate School (OCS), which is located at the Coast Guard Academy in Connecticut. Applicants to OCS must be on active or Reserve duty, have a baccalaureate or higher degree, or be senior active-duty personnel (E-5 or above) with at least four years of service with the Coast Guard.

Officer Candidate School is a challenging seventeen-week course of instruction. Much of the program focuses on the specialized knowledge and training that Coast Guard officers need to perform their leadership duties.

A graduate of the OCS program is commissioned an ensign in the Coast Guard and is required to serve on active duty for at least three years. Cadets at the Coast Guard Academy are commissioned as officers at graduation. A new officer's capabilities and the needs of the Coast Guard will determine whether he or she will be assigned to a ship, to flight training, or to a shore operation.

There are ten ranks and ten alphanumeric pay grades, designated by the letter O, for commissioned Coast Guard officers. The names of the ranks, from Ensign to Admiral, correspond with those used by the Navy. An eleventh rank, Fleet Admiral, is only used in times of war.

As elsewhere in the armed forces, warrant officers are generally highly trained specialists in a given field (usually technical). Warrant officers usually do not have command or staff positions. The three warrant officer pay grades are W-2, W-3, and W-4.

SALARY
AND BENEFITS

THERE ARE FINANCIAL, EDUCATIONAL, and personal benefits available to U.S. Coast Guard personnel. The benefits for active-duty personnel differ somewhat from those of Reserve personnel.

BENEFITS

ENLISTED ACTIVE DUTY

1. Full-time salary
2. Thirty days paid vacation annually
3. Retirement income plus savings program
4. Free medical, dental, and hospital care
5. Low-cost post exchange (PX) (department store) and commissary (grocery store) privileges
6. Low-cost life insurance
7. Extra income, including allowances for subsistence and housing

Boatswain mates (*from left*) Jason C. Jackson, Dave Phillips, and Ted F. Strzalkowski cruise through the waters of the North Arabian Sea after delivering mail to a Coast Guard cutter stationed there.

COAST GUARD RESERVE

1. Part-time salary
2. Low-cost life and dental insurance
3. Retirement insurance

Members of the Coast Guard Auxiliary are volunteer civilians. They are not obligated to fulfill any military service and therefore do not receive pay or benefits.

SALARY

The salary of each member of the active-duty Coast Guard or the Coast Guard Reserve depends on his or her rank and pay grade. Salary increases with each promotion, as well as with each cost of living allowance (COLA).

EDUCATIONAL BENEFITS

The Coast Guard provides its personnel with facilities and financial means to get ahead in their careers and improve their personal lives by continuing their education. Advanced job training and leadership courses are also available to Coast Guard personnel. The Coast Guard offers scholarships that provide funds for college, apprentice-ships, or vocational training.

THE MONTGOMERY GI BILL

The Montgomery GI Bill (MGIB) is a generously endowed government program that helps personnel in all branches of

Coastguardsmen stationed on the *Hamilton* board a fishing vessel off the coast of Alaska. The *Hamilton* was the first Coast Guard high endurance cutter assigned to homeland security in Arctic waters.

the U.S. military attain their educational goals. Coast Guard personnel on active duty, as well as certain members of the Reserve, are eligible to apply for this program, which is intended to finance a college education.

Active-duty Coast Guard personnel who wish to take advantage of the Montgomery Bill must enlist for a term of at least three years; as of 2009 the amount of the grant was nearly $40,000. To qualify for the grant, Coast Guard personnel must contribute $100 each month to the Montgomery program during the first year of service.

Coast Guard reservists who want to apply for the Montgomery Bill must enlist for six years and maintain a record of satisfactory drill attendance. Reservists are eligible for up to thirty-six months of educational assistance.

READY FOR TODAY, PREPARING FOR TOMORROW

Service in the U.S. Coast Guard or the Coast Guard Reserve carries great prestige and can lead to a satisfying career. The Coast Guard Auxiliary is a great option for those interested in helping the Coast Guard, but do not want to commit to military service. Information on service in the U.S. Army, Navy, Air Force, or Marine Corps is available in the other books in this series, which explain the opportunities and requirements of each branch.

ACRONYM GLOSSARY

ADC	Assignment Data Card
ASVAB	Armed Services Vocational Aptitude Battery
CBP	Customs and Border Patrol
COLA	Cost of living allowance
DEP	Delayed Entry Program
E	Enlisted, in pay grade designation
ICE	Immigration and Customs Enforcement
MGIB	Montgomery GI Bill
MITE	Minority Introduction to Engineering
NCO	Noncommissioned officer
NRC	National Response Center
O	Officer, in pay grade designation
OCS	Officer Candidate School
PT	Physical training
PX	Post exchange; also called base exchange (BX)
SPARs	Women's Reserve of the U.S. Coast Guard
USCG	United States Coast Guard
USCGA	United States Coast Guard Academy
USCIS	U.S. Citizenship and Immigration Services
W	Warrant officer, in pay grade designation

FURTHER INFORMATION

WEBSITES

The official website of the U.S. Coast Guard
www.uscg.mil

The website of the U.S. Coast Guard Reserve
www.uscg.mil/reserve

The website of the U.S. Coast Guard Auxiliary
www.cgaux.org

The website of the U.S. Coast Guard for new and potential recruits
www.gocoastguard.com

The website of the U.S. Coast Guard Academy
www.cga.edu

SELECTED BIBLIOGRAPHY

Axelrod, Alan, and Charles Phillips. *Macmillan Dictionary of Military Biography*. New York: Macmillan, 1998.

Chambers, John Whiteclay, II, ed. *Oxford Companion to American Military History*. New York: Oxford University Press, 1999.

Holmes, Richard, ed. *Oxford Companion to Military History*. New York: Oxford University Press, 2001.

INDEX

EDWARD F. DOLAN is the author of more than 120 published nonfiction books. His most recent book for Marshall Cavendish Benchmark is *George Washington* in the series Presidents and Their Times. Mr. Dolan is a California native and currently resides near San Francisco.